WOLVERHAMPTON IN TH
1930s & '40s

by

Elizabeth Rees

Front cover: Queen Square during the Second World War.

Published by Hendon Publishing Co. Ltd., Hendon Mill, Nelson, Lancashire.
Text © Elizabeth Rees, 1988
Printed by Fretwell & Cox Limited, Goulbourne Street, Keighley, West Yorkshire BD21 1PZ.

1. Victoria Street in about 1931. Note the huge sign advertising 'Talkies' at the Hippodrome Theatre in Queen Square, which showed films for less than a year in 1931–2. The first film shown was *Derelict* starring George Bancroft and William Boyd. Beatties store, rebuilt in 1929, can be seen on the left of the picture.

2. Lichfield Street, from Princes Square, in about 1935. This was the site of Britain's first automatic traffic light, experimented with in 1927 and installed permanently in 1928. Originally there was also a policeman on point duty to ease the flow of traffic but by the mid '30s the lights were obviously sufficiently familiar not to require this. The tangle of trolley bus wires was also a familiar sight in Wolverhampton's streets, introduced from 1923.

3. North Street in the '30s. The wall of the Market Hall can be seen on the left of the picture while the right-hand side of the road, now occupied by the Civic Hall and telephone exchange had a range of interesting old buildings. Most significant, next to the Town Hall, is the prebendary house of Monmore, a gabled Jacobean building which by this time had acquired shop fronts on the ground floor. Behind the tree was another fine old building formerly used as the Liberal Club. The Old Mitre and Jessops Hotel stood next to one another followed by Cartlidge Bros, 'Ye Olde Mangle Shoppe'. Another old gabled building, divided into two shops, is in the foreground of the picture, together with the Education Offices, formerly the Bluecoat School.

4. The corner of Chapel Ash and Clifton Street in about 1930. The corner premises were converted into a bank in that year and are still used for that purpose. The tyre dealers are also still in the same location, as are the workshops of W. Hopcraft, monumental masons. The principal change in the last fifty years has been in the volume of traffic using Chapel Ash, now one of Wolverhampton's busiest routes.

5.   The foundation stone of the Wolverhampton and Staffordshire Technical College, now the Polytechnic, was laid by Prince George on 7th October 1931. This photograph was taken in 1932 when the building was almost complete.

6. & 7.   Celebrated local character Sergeant-Major John Stratford died on 16th January 1932, at the age of 102. A veteran of the Indian Mutiny, Sergeant-Major Stratford had been saluted in 1928 by the 14th/20th Hussars outside his house in Newhampton Road. He is pictured as an old man wearing his old uniform and campaign medals, still displaying a military bearing.

8.   Princes Square, looking towards Stafford Street, in the '30s. The George Hotel
was rebuilt in 1930 to take on its modern appearance.

9. & 10.   The Odeon Cinema, Skinner Street, pictured in the course of construction in 1937, and in about 1944. It opened on 11th September 1937 and could seat nearly 2,000 people. It was converted into a triple-screen cinema in 1973 and is now a bingo club.

11. Chas Hales' butcher's shop in Heath Town at Christmas 1931. The Hales' family business was at Cannock Market but Charles set up his own shop at Heath Town. As well as butchering he was well known as a sporting man and in 1967 set up a World Record in Tokyo for swallowing 52 eggs in 52 seconds.

12. Dudley Street in about 1930. The Kings Head public house is on the left of the picture next to the Central Arcade, opened in 1902. The group of shops in the centre of the photograph was newly built in 1927.

CIVIC HALL. WOLVERHAMPTON
BUILT 1938

13. & 14.   The Wolverhampton Civic Hall, designed by E.D. Lyons and L. Israel of Ilford, was opened in 1938, some eighteen years after the idea of a concert hall was first put forward. The opening ceremony was followed by a civic ball for 900 guests with music provided by Jack Hylton and his Band.

15. & 16. The new Lea Road Congregational Church opened on 7th March 1932, replacing a school-chapel which had served since 1905. The opening ceremony was performed by Mrs James Thompson of Ludstone Hall, Claverley, and the service was conducted by Reverend S.M. Berry, secretary of the Congregational Union of England and Wales, and son of Dr Charles Berry, the famous Wolverhampton preacher and writer.

17.   Wolverhampton Wanderers reached the final of the FA Cup in 1939 but were beaten 4–1 by Portsmouth. They were not to win it until ten years later when they beat Leicester City 3–1. In the picture Stan Cullis, later Wolves' manager, introduces the players to King George VI before the 1939 final. Tom Galley is shaking hands with the King.

18. & 19.   The Town Hall and Queen Square decorated for the Jubilee of King George V in 1935.

20.   Buxton & Bonnett's shop in Dudley Street in 1933. The shop front was remodelled in the mid '20s.

21. & 22.   The Westminster Bank building in Princes Square in course of alteration in 1930. The London Paperhangings Stores also took advantage of the general refurbishing to acquire a new shop front.

23.   Queen Square in about 1932, with the Hippodrome Theatre at the centre of the picture.

24.   Dudley Street in the early '30s. Many of the large multiple stores modernised their shop fronts at about this time giving the street a more unified and up-to-date appearance, and this photograph appeared in the Wolverhampton Industrial Development Association handbook for 1932.

25.   Wolverhampton's built-up area expanded markedly in the 1930s, particularly to the north of the town. The Bushbury Arms was built at Low Hill in about 1929 to serve the growing number of inhabitants in the area.

26.   The South Staffordshire Permanent Building Society, Princess Street, decorated for the coronation of King George VI in 1937. The building itself was newly erected in 1933, incorporating the rebuilding of the Talbot Inn next door.

27.   Children of Field Street, Springfield, celebrate the coronation of King George VI in 1937 with a street party.

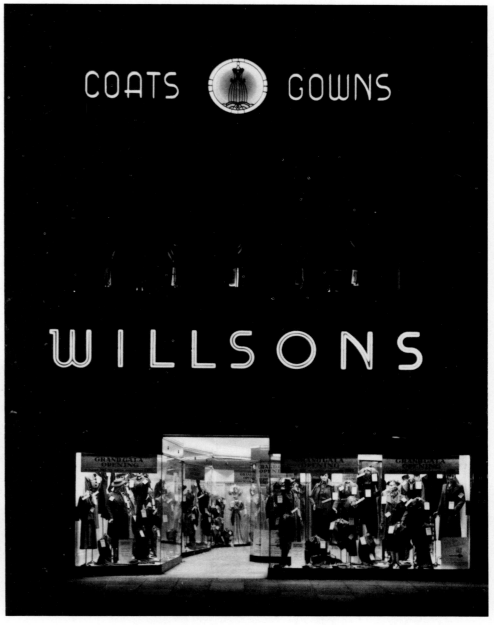

28.   J W Hughes' bakery, 19 Victoria Street, in July 1932. The girls were in costume for a stall at the Old English Fayre at the annual Floral Fête.

29.   In complete contrast, the ultra-modern new façade of Wilson's dress-shop in Dudley Street in 1937.

30. The Gaumont Palace Cinema, Snow Hill, pictured in 1934. This cinema was opened in 1932 on the site of the old Agricultural Hall and was Wolverhampton's first 'super-cinema'. It closed in 1973, one of the last events being a live show with Cliff Richard.

31.   Wolverhampton's Library service expanded in the '30s to match the growing population of the town. The first branch library was at Low Hill, opened in 1930.

32.   The Hospital Library Service began in May 1939; William Beeston, borough librarian, watches Joan Hughes, Muriel Wilkes and Doris Jones give out the first books at the Royal Hospital.

33.   Worcester Street in the 1940s. The Georgian buildings on the left of the road contrast with the modern block on the right-hand side built in 1927.

34. & 35.   The Wolverhampton Gas Company's new showroom
was built in 1939 to replace their original Victorian premises.

36.   Queen Square pictured during the war. Prince Albert's statue, erected in 1866, exhorts passers-by to buy National Savings Ceritficates while the bank advertises National War Bonds. The lamp standards in the centre of the picture normally bore directional signs, but they were taken down for the duration to frustrate enemy parachutists.

37.   Fallings Park Methodist Church opened in 1936 and replaced a wooden hut which had been in use since 1908. The new building was erected in record time with the foundation stone laid on 13th June 1936 and opened for worship on 22nd October.

38.   Market Street in the early '30s. These shops had just been built in the style which can still be seen throughout Wolverhampton town centre. The adjoining land was being sold by Wolverhampton Corporation and would itself shortly be filled up with new shops.

39.   The Giffard Arms, Victoria Street, was
rebuilt in Gothic style in about 1930. A similar
style was used by the same brewery for the
Dudley Arms in Dudley Street, but this façade is
now covered with a modern shop-front.

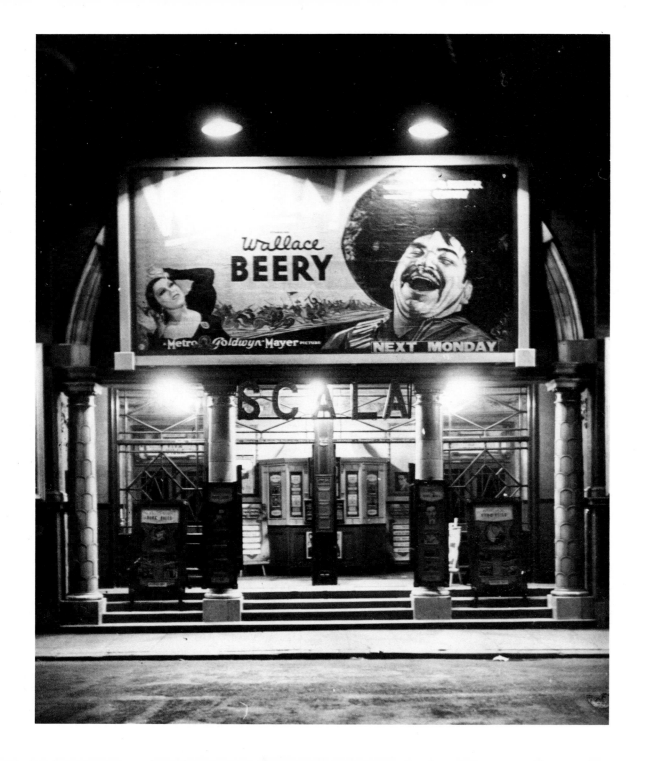

40. The Scala Cinema, Worcester Street, in October 1934. This was one of Wolverhampton's older cinemas, opened as the Picturedrome in 1913, but forced to upgrade in the '30s to compete with the luxurious new picture palaces. It closed as a cinema in 1956 and has since had a chequered history as a ballroom and a bingo hall.

41. Bilston Street in 1941. This Queen Anne house was later converted into shops and was demolished in 1953.

42.   Sandbagging the offices of Tettenhall Urban District Council in 1939 against possible bomb damage. In fact a number of bombs did fall on Tettenhall, but the offices remain unscathed and are now used in part by the Tettenhall Regis Library.

43.   *Everyman* at St Peter's Church on 2nd July
1941. This morality play was produced by church
groups in the town and Reverend J. Vernon
Twigg played Death. Several hundred people
stood in the market square to watch the play,
which ran for three nights.

44. & 45.   Tatlows in Cleveland Road, bombed on 30th July 1942. This glass and plumbers' merchants adjoined the bus depot and seven double-decker buses were destroyed in the same raid.

46. The Grove, Tettenhall Wood, the home of H. T. Fullwood was destroyed by a bomb in 1940. It was rebuilt after the war in a modern style but has since been demolished and a private hospital built on the site.

47. Bomb damage in Bilston on 20th August 1940.

48.   A plane crash damaged houses in Parkfield Road on 21st July 1941. The two Czech members of the plane crew were killed in the crash, which set the roofs of three houses on fire, but none of the occupants was injured.

49. A patriotic wartime window display at Marks and Spencer, Dudley Street.

50.   Another patriotic display at Beatties Department Store in about 1942, after the United States
had entered the war. Stalin's Russia was another of the allies honoured in this window.
Montgomery's picture was displayed in the next.

51.   Repatriated prisoners of war visiting women voluntary workers at the Manor House,
Tettenhall, in 1943. They were ? Rhodes, G. Aspray, A.C. Powis, W.E. Price, S. Doughty, B.
Eastelow, H. Jones, W. Slater, G. Kirkbridge and W. Hill.

52.   Wolverhampton Wanderers won the War League Cup in 1942 after playing two legs against Sunderland with an aggregate score of 6–3. Seventy-five thousand spectators watched the final at Molineux. In the picture Tom Galley, Wolves' Captain, accepts the cup from the King and Queen. As the tournament was never played again this trophy is still in Wolves' possession.

53.   Street parties were held all over the town to celebrate VE Day in 1945. This one was in Park Village.

54.   The VE Day street party in Cardiff Street, Penn Fields. Entertainment was provided by a barrel-organ, which can be seen on the left of the picture.

55.   VE Day celebrations in Alma Street, Heath Town. Causeway Lake School is on the left of the picture.

56.   Wolverhampton celebrated its centenary as a borough in 1948 with a number of events including an exhibition
of local industries at the Civic Hall.

57.   The Duke of Edinburgh visited Wolverhampton in December 1948 as part of the borough centenary celebrations. After arriving by train at the Low Level Station the Duke visited the Civic Hall and two local factories, Courtaulds and Fisher Bearings. The photograph shows the procession from the Town Hall to the Civic Hall with, from left to right: Mr W. H. Cartwright Sharp, the Recorder; Mr J. Brock Allon, the town clerk; the Duke; Ald. H. E. Lane, the mayor; Lt-Gen Sir Frederick Browning; Lt-Col F. L. Martin of the First Battalion, South Staffordshire Regiment; and the mayoress.